PART CREATION MYTH, PART PROPHECY, Kristin Bock's *Glass Bikini* stitches together the fabrics of our dystopian present, reminding us of our culpability and power in this grand, human experiment. These often darkly humorous poems guide readers into dreamscapes and underworlds that are ominously contemporary. From a looking-glass planet, we peer back at our own homes and see the news as a horror movie. There is the sickening feeling that something has gone terribly wrong. Monsters prowl here inspired as much by Sarah Kane as Mary Shelley. We hold a tiny prehistoric horse in our paws. We are masochistic voodoo dolls traipsing hand in hand through grisliness and the sublime. If there is any hope in this nightmarish proliferation of cyborgs and militia, it lies within the liberating powers of the feminine. *Glass Bikini* is both mirror and warning, asking us to see our own strange and terrifying shapes, the monsters we have helped create, and the ones we have become.

GLASS BIKINI

GLASS BIKINI

Kristin Bock

TUPELO PRESS

North Adams, Massachusetts

Library of Congress Control Number: 2021934637

ISBN-13: 978-1-946482-55-6

Cover and text design by Ann Aspell.
Cover Photo Credit: ESA/Hubble & NASA

First paperback edition November 2021

Tupelo Press
P.O. Box 1767
North Adams, Massachusetts 01247
(413) 664-9611 / Fax: (413) 664-9711
editor@tupelopress.org / www.tupelopress.org

Tupelo Press is an award-winning independent literary press that publishes fine fiction, non-fiction, and poetry in books that are a joy to hold as well as read. Tupelo Press is a registered 501(c) (3) non-profit organization, and we rely on public support to carry out our mission of publishing extraordinary work that may be outside the realm of the large commercial publishers. Financial donations are welcome and are tax deductible.

For my brother, Stephen—
my other heart

Contents

III. WONDERLAND

IV. UNCANNY VALLEYS

V. THE LOOKING-GLASS PLANET

The Truth, is Bald, and Cold—

—Emily Dickinson

OVERCOME

And it came to pass, art became extinct. Still, we flocked to museums and stared into barren rooms. Look! Someone would exclaim. *There's a man rolling around on the floor, acting like an unbalanced washing machine, knocking into things and coughing up wet rags. Isn't it horrifying? Oh yes, excruciating, someone would yell out. People whizzed in Duchamp's missing fountain.* They blew each other like whistles where *L'Origine du monde* used to hang. They wept under restroom signs for what might have been. People shredded their clothes, oozed from chandeliers. Entire floors wailed, cackled, threw their necks back so far, they almost snapped. A child said, *Look, those red velvet ropes clearly symbolize our happiness,* and another child said, *oh no, our happiness symbolizes those red velvet ropes.* And thus began the gnashing of hair and the pulling of teeth that lasted for the rest of the unknown world.

Before Birds

Monstrum praecessit Monstro

— Pliny the Elder

CREATION MYTH

First, the armature, thick cable for legs, thinner for the trunk, arms, and head. The ideal monster is 8 hands tall. A fashion monster, 8-1/2. A heroic monster, at least 9. Now, ask yourself, what would you like to make and how big are your hands? Start with the skeleton; add ligaments, tendons, the long muscles of the body. Think origin and insertion. Pound out the skin until you see through it. Laugh a nervous laugh. Add a thumb of oblivion (your own thumb will do), a whisper of gunpowder, a box of static, a bucket of mud. Then, find the ribbon within the figure, the gesture at its center and pull.

SNUFF POEM

I have a monster. It has a hole in its belly. You can see straight through to the other side. Sometimes, I reach into its cage and put my hand through the hole. The monster doubles over and cries for a time. I let it out, ride it around like a donkey. I tie feathers to its neck and bid it sing like a waterfall. I point. I laugh. I eat a rabbit on the floor. The monster's eyes are dark and bottomless. Like stars turned inside out. I hood it. I leash it. I broomstick it. But no matter what I try, each night, thousands of soldiers collect at the hole and stare out at me. They all have the same face. They pour from the monster's belly, tumble over each other like mice from a silo. I press my palm to the hole, but they shoulder through. By daybreak, the army holds me at gunpoint.

EVERYTHING COMING UP RIFLES

Rifles are pushing up in the garden. The orchard is clacking with rifles. Bouquets of rifles adorn our tables. Shadows on the floorboards are rifles. Sidewalks are cobbled with rifles. Our fences, rifles. All the crosses in the graveyard are rifles. The church bell's tongue is a long, black rifle. Coloring books are thick with rifles. Rifles falling from the clouds. Rifles clogging our chimneys. Rafts of rifles jamming the river. Our lost lovers are rifles. Our silhouettes, rifles. Our arms, rifles. The trees are enormous rifles no one can wrap their rifles around.

THE GIFT

In the beginning, there were Flame Trees. People took particles from the Flame Trees and swallowed them like pills. They spun a fine golden thread from their mouths. Soon, all the pants in the city sparkled with golden thread. The hats in the city were golden thimbles and flashy golden saucers. When the dresses in the city began to spin into golden tornados the People went blind. They slid on their bellies in search of the Flame Trees, but the Flame Trees bent down and burned them. That night, the People curled into a cavernous sleep of earthly things.

In the morning, trees in the shapes of beautiful dark vaginas had grown higher than the spires of churches.

HOW RABBITS FINALLY TOOK OVER THE WORLD

Some time after the extinction of whales, babies were born in pieces. Lungs, feet, spleens all separate and in heaps. We dumped the remains of our babies in the woods, in the fields and into the seas. To our dismay, the single parts arose and animated. Heads without necks rolled around trying to connect with other parts. Hearts, arms, and tongues crept over the Earth in grotesque parades. Organs and limbs clumped together and survived for a time. One species sported a head, a lung, and a huge, inverted foot with eight toes. It hopped around at an astonishing speed, and in inclement weather, it raised its foot above its head like an umbrella. Herds of one-eyed livers slithered over hill and dale until the species that resembled a crab (but was really a hand with a mouth in its palm) gobbled up all the one-eyed livers. It went on like this for millions of years, hybrid devouring hybrid. Until one day, scores of baby ears nested inside each other to form beautiful fleshy dahlias. Rabbits all over the world thrived on the soft, sweet lobes. Rabbits of the fields and of the ice and the air grew as large as humans, were born whole and forever tender.

BUNNY WOMAN

Her ears are blue and pink inside. She sports a blue fur bustier and big satin bowtie. She is aglow with bows. What a luxury to be aglow with bows! I wish I were aglow with bows. I wish I were blue and furry and pink inside. The end of a white horse trots out of the picture, waving goodbye, goodbye with its immaculate handkerchief. By nightfall, a monkey in a suit drifts away. On the horizon, gold balloons bounce up invisible ladders. I wish I were gold and weightless and heaven bound. Everything is moving away from Bunny Woman. Even the fireflies and the radio signals. Even the cow dangling from that airship is trying to run. As if there were a bomb planted in Bunny Woman's fur. As if you can no longer trust the friendliest places on the planet.

PLUTO

Come bomb cookers, come poison makers, come girl biters, come water boarders, come dress torchers, come lone gunmen with the sidereal eyes, come rageful lovers, come blue wall silencers, come baby shakers, come fag haters, come proud proud boys, come serial chokers, come Demiciders, come bury-her-up-to-her-neck-and-stone-her stoners, come high drivers, come joyful lynchers, come whore splitters, come blue washers, come Genderciders, come vehicle rammers, come good old-fashioned back stabbers—there's a place for you here, inside my vacuous core of ice and ash.

BROKEN MIRROR

Three is slippery staircase.
Two is a head-on collision.
One is a burning kitchen.

When I count my reflection
in shards of glass, a small light
pitches in the skin of everything.

It's four in the morning,
the electric hour.
And this is no accident—

this is what will be.
There is little warning
when the countdown begins.

A great mirror falls
and you will wake
just seconds before.

Into the Woods

if I cannot inspire love, I will cause fear

—MARY WOLLSTONECRAFT SHELLEY

GASLIGHTER

A friend makes me a beautiful handbag in all of my favorite colors—rusty orange and chocolate polka dots embroidered with golden thread. When I stroll through town, I get a lot of compliments and feel very special. The next day, even though I didn't put anything in the bag, it starts to get heavy. When I bring it back to my friend's house, she turns it upside down and out pours a pyramid of brilliant jewels I have stolen. They are blindingly beautiful! I'm surprised because I don't remember stealing the jewels, but I'm so grateful for the beautiful bag, I give them to her. After a time, the bag becomes heavy again. When my friend empties it, out falls more jewels and a severed hand. I realize it's my hand and start to scream. *There, there*, she says, *you've still got your other hand. Here, let me paint your fingernails a beautiful arctic blue.* She holds my hand in hers with such tenderness I start to cry. *Of course, you're right. Thank you*, I say, and leave with my beautiful bag in my one beautiful hand. Year after year I empty the bag of body parts on her couch, until one day it's too heavy to lift. I drag it down the street by my teeth. *I am hobbled and ugly*, I say to my friend. *No*, she says, *you are a like a rare bird who flies without wings, who sings without a beak. Yes, of course, you're right*, I say. *It's very dark in your house today*, I say, *and I can hardly hear you. I think I'm inside the bag. No*, she says, *you're sitting here right beside me. It's just your head inside the bag and it's beautiful.*

COMPOUND

Come stand in the garden. Let the soft rain rinse you. Line up with the others. Hold hands. Now, kiss. Imagine your mind is a blue rose, a rose rinsed clean. Hide in the bushes. Wait for the little black stars to squeak by. Step on them. Stamp on them. Some will feel like urchins under your feet. They will whisper terrible things. Step on them harder. They will cry out. They will have your mother's voice. Run. Catch the stars and squeeze until they burst. They will be slippery. Their black oil will leak into the earth. Now your hands are dirty. They're filthy. Go back to your spot in the garden and stand like a flower. Do not move until your skin becomes blue and clean and cold. Take off your dress. You are dirty inside. Open your legs to the rain. Your mind unfolds like a blue rose. Now you've been bad. Very bad. Today you will not eat. Today you will stamp on the little black stars until your feet are raw. The stars will squirt and whimper. They will sound like your father crying in the shed. Step on him. Make him cry harder. He is dirty. Your mother is dirty. Come to me. Come to us. Open your legs. Let us rinse you. My brain is as big as a car. My brain is as big as a mountain range. I will bend my fat red brain over you like a blood-soaked rose. I will sing to you and wash you and starve you and love you like no other. Now go back to the garden and plant yourself where you belong.

THE KILLING SHOW

For a long time, I watched a boy on the beach sneak up on a wounded seabird. He stepped slowly, gently as if through a maze of mines. When, finally, he towered over the bird floundering on its side, and pelted it with small, smooth stones. *You'll like me*, yelled the boy. *You'll like me!* As the bird cried louder, the boy dropped heavier stones. The sun leaked. The waves claimed the bird and, as our shadows grew larger, we all grew smaller.

B-MOVIE

It's a hot, steamy night. In the distance, coyotes fight for the last housecat. A scientist, played by my father, accidently drops a maddening fluid onto a plate of Wonder Bread. The food begins to quiver and grows to the size of my Pinto. It resembles a huge lump of pulsating liver and immediately eats my father and half of me. My lower half is completely gone. I drag my entrails through the house and out onto the lawn, smashing gnomes and pulling my hair clean out. Neighbors flee to the deepest, TV-lit corners of their converted basements. And suddenly, splayed in the pachysandra, I notice I've grown an amorphous, bloody bottom-half and a voracious hunger. All night, pitchforks and torches taunt me, but I just open my giant, gelatinous body and swallow the hunting parties whole. Next, I roll down Main Street and into the arcade, consuming my childhood friends, roller-skates and all. Finally, I reach the outer edge of town, where the power plant glows, and where the heroine, played by my mother, kills me with one hundred thousand kisses, putting an end to anything born from wonder.

A SNOWMAN IS CRYING TEARS OF FIRE

A snowman is crying tears of fire. They burn straight through his mittens. *Stigmata,* the snowman mouths to the boy, turning his palms to the moon. *Hot coals for eyes, you know.* The boy nods. *We are alike, you and I,* says the snowman—*with our corny hats, just waiting for the world to knock us down and laugh. No,* says the boy, *I am more like my father,* and knocks the snowman's head off. *Why did you hurt me,* the snowman asks, his mouth half-crushed, full of snow and stones. *My father says a freshly severed head will always try to bite the earth,* says the boy. *I see,* says the snowman, *and rage never targets its intended.*

INVITATION

On Monday, Satan takes out the garbage of the world.
On Tuesday, Satan takes out the garbage of the world.
On Wednesday, Satan takes out the garbage of the world.
On Thursday, Satan takes out the garbage of the world.
On Friday, Satan takes out the garbage of the world.
On Saturday, Satan takes out the garbage of the world.

On Sunday, Satan folds his dark wings, turns on
the little lamp above his desk and writes:

Dear Dayside Creatures

I am a boy who lives in the woods.
I'll leave the moon on
all night among the leaves.

BARN BURNING

I was sixteen, driving
home from sweet wine

and fucking in the far fields.
When I opened the door

to the burning barn,
my lips, raw from kissing,

stung, swelled from the heat.
I was the devil

staring
from the edge of the woods

at over one hundred horses
fleeing from their stalls,

my long red hair
snaking in hot wind.

Out of the smoke,
a mare walked up to me,

slowly, as if she knew me—
as if we weren't on fire.

UNCANNY VALLEYS

When you pass a mannequin in a store window, and she looks exactly like your mother when she was young, without hands.

When you see sandbags about your size.

When, at night, the closet door left open like a coffin.

When you run up to the edge of a cliff, lie on your belly and look down at the tops of trees for the first time.

When you see a mannequin that looks just like your father but has no sex parts.

When his face through warbled glass.

When your whole family goes hunting for garnets and the rock face looks like blood spatter.

When you have sex for the first time, look in a mirror and are surprised you are still a girl.

When something freshly torn out twitches.

When dragged by your ankles down a rock face by your father.

When dragged by your ankles anywhere.

When no one comforts you crying in the woods and, at the same time, you are looking down at yourself crying in the woods.

When years later, you are chased through the woods by a boy you love, or think you love, and cry for an angel with the face of your mother.

When you finally grow up and just finish fucking someone you think you love, and shit pours from their mouth.

When you find yourself on stage next to a stripper barking at you on all fours like a dog.

When everyone is laughing.

When you bare your teeth like a dog.

When the tops of trees are beautiful for a few seconds, and then they are not beautiful, not beautiful ever again.

When the cigarette hanging from your father's bottom lip looks like a skinny white girl.

When you catch your reflection in dirty toilet water.

When dragged down a rock face, not just a few inches, but the length of many twelve-year-old girls strung together.

When you dream you are being crucified on a mountain and look down on the roof of your home.

When a heavy branch crashes through a tangle of branches and hits the ground with a thud and, for a split second, you think it's your mother.

When dusk casts a green light on your veined hands and you wonder if you've finally turned.

When years later, peeling eggs in the kitchen, a bleating goat startles the afternoon you thought you were happy inside.

When you can no longer tell if you were ripped from the trees or the trees were ripped from you.

When a maddening fluid takes you by the ankles.

When your hipbones are peeled eggs.

When a bleating goat.

When the animals of the forest swivel their eyes and ears away from the direction of the cliff.

MY FATHER'S CHIAROSCURO

Each day, I watched him paint the porcelain doll. Stripped down, cocked to the side, one arm stretched out to the viewer. Her glass eyes extracted years ago. A wide hole on top where hair should be. I wanted to hold her. She looked nothing like my others in yellow ruffles and curls. All those holes. All those ways in. Once, I peered down inside her head—some balls of dust, a pearl button, a crushed cigarette, a few dried bees. I was still a child when I came to understand my father's long shadow at the close of day. Her nakedness and her reaching.

MY FATHER'S PAINT-BOX

The color of grief is wolf

Forgiveness, sailcloth

Argument, oxbow—

(There is a whisper
of gunpowder in every color)

I am a wolf
wrapped in sailcloth

laid below
the hanging oxbow

GET BACK

At the party, my mother curls into a set of ovaries and vein-blue tubes. A shiny dark bag blooms from her mouth and turns her inside out. Everyone is laughing. I pick her up and carry her upstairs. She is slippery and making a sound like static. I find my brother lying in the hall. One eye whirling in its socket. His arms and legs are fleshy knobs, red and swollen like the walls. I drop my mother, and everybody laughs. It's just so funny. She slumps over and throbs in the corner. My brother slouches toward her. I try to grab him by the stumps, but they are slick from the forewaters. I keep dropping him in the rising muck. Everyone is convulsively laughing. We can't stop. We slip, go under. It's hilarious. All of us grabbing onto each other. All of us ill-made, laughing, and trying to get back inside.

THE INSIDE-OUT

Sometimes, that dark specter we imagine loving us back through all the years grows so heavy inside, it's hard to carry around, hard to bear through the dream of the inside-out, where the wind whistles through the bones of birds choking on their own feathers, on all that once lifted them up and out, the dream where your heart finally grows so large it breaks through bone, muscle, sinew and skin to recollect whole and wet on the outside. And you have to go on with your life—to the office and the gym and the day-glow market in your bloody nightclothes, as if no one can see it beating you down.

ON THE DAY OF YOUR WEDDING

On the day of your wedding,
I'm beating a dead monkey

on the cathedral stairs. I'm wearing
my hat with the horns, a gown

of red arrows that point straight
down. On the day of your wedding,

I'm riding a carousel horse
in a glass bikini cut

from the radioactive plains
of the Forbidden Zone.

Covered in katydids, licking
Oblivion from a dinner plate

with my gold-leafed tongue,
sitting and speaking of love

as if it could save us.
Here is my full set of wax teeth.

Here is your dress like a bandage.
Here, my monkey paws.

THE ISLAND OF ZERRISSENHEIT

The island pulls at you every moment
without rest. You'll be rent into pieces,

torn apart by sorrow. The only creatures
that escape are birds. They say even mermaids

go mad, biting the bottoms of boats
in the bay. In early morning, you can see them

dragging themselves to shore. Mermaids
with mouths bloody, full of splinters.

Mermaids blinded by their own blue hands.
I came to this island after the death of a friend.

Actually, she did not die. She's still alive
but I am dead to her. The island told me

this is a special kind of sorrow. A sorrow
with a light inside that never goes out—

an inverse lighthouse at the bottom
of a sea. They say your hands fall off first,

most likely at the shore where it's windiest.
No, those are not starfish scattered on the sand.

They are hands curling in on themselves, making
little nests on the beach. Sometimes, they scuttle

away to cut off other hands. The abandoned
always retreat or lash out, but never make it free.

The island has three rules: Never try to warm
the freshly dead. Never dismember a mermaid

by moonlight. Never, ever, fall in love
with a bird. I've come to know the difference

between sadness and grief. Sadness
is the knell of a bell on a buoy at night,

riding the swells. Grief is a boat
exactly the size and shape of the sea.

I see you approaching the island, friend,
but can no longer wave you in.

WONDERLAND

I must have the fat boy or some other monster or something new.

—P.T. BARNUM

SCULPTURE GARDEN

Two iron tongues
Tied in knots

A muffled trumpet
Called God's Ear

Plastic catapult

Hot-pink guillotine

The world plugged with swords

By sundown, a giant pair
Of scissors

Clicks quickly up the street

IN BACK OF THE LIQUOR STORE

When I turn the corner, a giant pair of scissors looms over me and leers as if I'm some kind of rodent. *I'm just looking for a place take a drink,* I say. *I'm road-weary and the heat is brutal.* The scissors glare in silence. I slip on my sunglasses. After a long pause, the scissors spin around on one leg, glide toward a pyramid of boxes. The clicking sound on the pavement shoots a welcome chill up my back. Its spine is straight and strong, unlike mine, which is full of eggshells. I watch it cut down the boxes. *Wow, that was deft,* I say. It pretends to ignore me, but I can tell it's glad for the praise. All afternoon, I have an uncontrollable urge to follow it, to reach out and touch it. I feel like a child's hair caught in the ropes of a swing, waiting for the wind and birds to have their way with me.

The sun shimmies like a tambourine over a tall brown city of recycling. A ruddy glow comes over the scissors. I find myself caressing its long svelte leg, working my way toward its inner thigh.

THE VAST WIDE-OPEN SPACE AREA

The Vast Wide-Open Space Area is the name of a park in my hometown. It was election year, and I was lounging under a walnut tree. Amid the danger of falling nuts, I met a man with a star-spangled shield, ten blue fingers and a pilly, red facemask. Together, on a park bench, we admired a map of Connecticut, noted great town names like Bethlehem and Bozrah. We noticed some black dots were larger than other black dots. He was very clever. He showed me the atlas had a face, and the United States was the forehead of the world. Imagine, for me he signed an entire book of checks! For the rest of the afternoon, we watched a man paint a flagpole from the bottom up. And so we parted—his silhouette punching a hole in the paper sky. My heart growing stars and stripes.

THE PRESIDENT'S DREAM

So, there I was with the kid, the board, the pitcher and the sopping cloth and it seemed like the right thing to do. It's monstrous speak! Then, a giant hand lifted me off the ship and threw me onto the arterial ground. Sometimes monsters are so big you can't see them. But you can feel their hands ragdolling you. There were wild ponies all around me, dark-eyed, stranded, their hoofs sunken into a long network of engorged veins. When the monster kissed me, I felt its dream in my mouth like so much water. Like so much blood. I couldn't breathe. There should be a word for a kiss between monsters. For stuck ponies. For kids in cages like that.

ALICE'S MMA FIGHT WITH THE PRESIDENT

Alice slips down a hole and falls feet first into a hot cup of entrails. She's guttin' it out with the President. First a calf-slicer, then an Achilles' lock, and then Alice gets him in a neck crank. But the President wriggles out, jumps high in the air and executes a sloppy double suplex into a rear naked choke, cutting the blood to Alice's head. She's bleeding from her nose. She's rolling around in her blood-damp nightclothes. She's trying to tap out, but the refs don't see her! Where are the refs?! Alice nibbles a mushroom, shrinks down, but the President just drops her in his pocket and thumbs her like a coin. Hissing with excitement, the audience hurls little cakes into the cage. When the President eats one, he grows bigger, mounts Alice, and grinds and pounds her into the mat. Alice grabs a cake, becomes a tall shovel, bonks him on the skull. The whole world shakes. They both fall flat on their sides, and she turns back into a girl. Quickly, the President gets her in a Peruvian Necktie. Blood leaks from her ear. She's trying to tap out, but the refs don't see her! Where are all the refs?! The President beats his chest and takes his victory lap. The whole stadium goes mad! They've turned into animals! They're slithering up the walls! They're wearing hats with horns, flying an old flag, and shouting *Eat or Be Eaten in Wonderland.*

IN THE SITUATION ROOM

Eat organic? *Yes, of course.* Good, because everything around here is slick with poison, you know. *I know.* How about your cleaning products? *What about them?* Are they friendly? *Yep.* No bleach in the house? *Nope.* Because you know if you mix chlorine with dish soap you get mustard gas, right? *Right.* World War I. *Yes, I know.* What about your water purification system? Does it filter out the ambiguities? *What exactly do you mean?* I mean, does your water purification system filter out particular particulates? *I guess so.* Good, because that stuff will turn your insides into wedding cake. *Oh!* What about your sunscreen? *What about it?* Does it use nanotechnology? *Um, I'll have to check.* Nanotechnology will eat your face in a matter of weeks. *Really?* Yeah, one day you'll wake up, go brush your teeth in the mirror, and realize you've wiped your face clean off. Your face will look straight up at you from the bottom of the sink and the cold water will still be running. Now, push the button.

ALL I WANT FOR NOW

Excuse me, sir, the zipper doesn't work. It doesn't fit me well. It fits me very well. I'll take it. Will you wrap it?

I'd like to see a pair of boots in the window. They're too wide. They pinch me. They fit me. I'll take them.

I also need a pair of slippers—gold, solid. One pair of gloves—burnt, kid.

Two dresses: one made of nail polish (Glitter Bomb), one of bullets.

I need them for a lecture, the lowlands, lockup. I need them by the end of the week, the day after tomorrow, tomorrow, tonight!

There's a button missing. Can you sew it on? Don't go. When will you bring it back?

Do you like my hat? I think it's cloying and sad, like an orphaned moon.

Glad to meet you! I met my destiny once. It came in the form of a maidenhead corsage. Was it bloody? Yes, yes it was! Do you have any of those?

Would you like a drink? A Q-tip? This fake nose?

Mind if I smoke? Your hands feel yellow, funny, solitary.

Are you busy this weekend? Tomorrow? Tonight? Here's my elbow.

Would you like to go to the masquerade, ice cream social, labooor-atory together?

Would you like to see my collapsible knife?

I'll wait for you in front of your hotel, under the linden tree,
the one with the heart-shaped leaves and almond-scented flowers.

Believe me. The pleasure was all mine.

MATCHMAKERS

Where does your monster sleep?

In a cage too small for him.

What does your monster's heart look like?

Like a child's teacup, small and full of blood.

What color is he?

Green, of course.

What does he eat?

Basically, nose to tail.

Cataracts?

Installed.

Fins?

Cauterized.

Fangs?

Restored.

Good. He's healthy then?

Yes, he takes ratfish liver oil—from a 300-million-year-old chimeric fish,
half-skate half-shark. It lives on the bottom of the sea and has the face of
a rat. Legend has it Norwegians would hang a ratfish by the head and the
liver oil would drip from its tail. They named the elixir "Gold of the Ocean"
and considered it a rare and precious gift. There are many other oils on the
market, but my monster prefers this one.

Excellent! He should make some fine little monsters. One last
question—does he have any *issues?*

Well, only if you count his fear of snow globes.

C'mon, snow globes?

Yes. They remind him of his childhood. His father was a snowman, and his
mother was an icicle. It snowed each and every day. His father cried tears of
fire for they begat a daughter named Wendy, who, after fifteen years of un-
forgivable acts of kindness, was sent to live among the moose.

Oh, forget it. My monster's not like that at all.

WELCOME TO THE DOLLAR STORE

We sell trilobites and gas masks. In the back, we have a real human pelvis, but it's two dollars. I'm dying a premature death since they added embalming fluid to the Slurpees. I'm in love with a young maiden adrift on a lily pad. She doesn't know I exist. She doesn't know anything exists (not even the solar system) and I like her that way. But what a vision! A vision of a vision! A real "floating eye" as they say. The moon on the pond is our escape pod to the center of the earth, where I will conduct a collision of planets, a revolution to call my own, endless feathers and finery. The Amber Room in heaven! Of course, there are no actual "rooms" in heaven. Only backyards with watchdogs, and boy are they mean!

WELCOME TO THE DOLLAR STORE: A TRANSLATION

Welcome! Can I interest you in an inspirational printed river stone?

No thanks. I'm a painter looking for a subject that epitomizes the post-modern dilemma.

What do you mean?

Well, we were meant to be simple animals, like this trilobite here, but something went terribly wrong and our brains grew too big, and now we're all freaking out and wearing gas masks.

I see. Well, how about this postcard of a young maiden adrift on a lily pad? She doesn't know the solar system exists and I like her that way. And what a vision! A vision of a vision! A real "floating eye" as they say.

I must admit, she is attractive and has a sweet naiveté about her, but I'm not into the kinderwhore thing.

In the back we have a real human pelvis, but it's two dollars.

Too macabre. Everyone wants to be entertained these days.

Gotcha. Well, how about this little hula girl? She's a lot of fun.

Too kitsch.

Right. Here's a bunch of blank name tags. Can't you paint those?

No, too self-referential.

But folks will want to write their names on them and won't be able to. Isn't that what you're getting at?

I guess so, but I want to make people think about what we're really made of.

Then how about this salt-shaker shaped like an outhouse?

Well, the excrementalists will like it.

This toy violin?

Too maudlin.

This Jesus nightlight?

Too meaningful. Let's put it this way. Sometimes at night, when I look out my window, I imagine throwing back the arrow of time. The air deadens. The trees darken slightly. The sky bends. All the gas and dust in the universe squeeze into smaller and smaller spheroids. Stars we've loved all our lives streak out of sight. Whole galaxies hurtle quietly away.

Ah-ha! The Big Bang in reverse. Sounds like a film.

Yeah, but I still don't know what to paint.

Set the film to a laugh track.

Ha-ha, very funny.

Here, try this.

A space-blue Slurpee? How so?

Simple. I'm dying a premature death since they added the embalming fluid.

Perfect! That should satisfy everyone.

POSTCARD FROM THE COFFIN

Everything was fine until the flood. Now my suit is ruined, caked with mud, especially the buttons, which I love. I remember someone at the wake whispered, *mother of Pearl*. I never met Pearl, though I would like to someday—My dearest Pearl, my snarl of light . . . How they used to shine, these buttons, even in the dark. Like promises. Like opals buried deep inside the moon.

UNCANNY VALLEYS

'Tis so appalling—it exhilarates—

—Emily Dickinson

FIELD TRIP TO THE WHITE HOUSE

The towering cookie chases the children. Its high, booming laugh echoes down dim corridors. Children scream and bawl when they glimpse its shiny black eyes and dripping red mouth. Nonetheless, parents drag their children through the maze by the wrists. But the Gingerbread Man is quicker than anyone can imagine. In a blink, he appears behind a child and grabs it by the neck. Some are never found. Some are found half-gobbled. Some are found with their eyes gouged and plugged with black buttons.

BELIEF IS A DEFAULT SETTING

From cadavers, grow new body parts. Use architecture to reanimate. Make rooms that have valves like doorways. Organs are buildings. Create a scaffold on which to plant cells, grow livers, ghost hearts. Wash out infected membranes. Replace damaged neural sections. Hook up nerves, the spinal cord. Make connections in a timely manner. A diamond knife chops the brain. Slice again and again. Scan with ion beams until tissue is digitalized. Copy. Download. Access Extreme Life Log Social Media Archive. Create Black Boxes of the Mind for good representation of personality. Switching points. Touchstones. Belief is a default setting. Activate the claustrum, the seat of consciousness. Wake as if from a long sleep. Bear to live with no tongue no hands no eyes. Dolls provide a framework, a narrative to explain your body. Feel a lack of control. See patterns in static, patterns in the stock market, in toast, in clouds, in invisible princesses. See meaning where there is none. Sense something ugly and festering in the heart of a friend. When there is none. A beast in the steaming leaves, a dark thing living in an old stove deep in the woods. When there is none.

TRANSHUMAN DEVOTION

When my children walk by, it will be like looking into the sun. Your children will have to bow their heads. My children's eyes will be the color of electric icebergs. Their eyes will be actual blue diamonds. They will come with built-in security systems, so your children won't pluck the gems from their faces when they sleep. Don't worry. My children will entertain your children. Symphonies from their cylinders! Poetry generators installed in their limbic systems. They will not need mouths. When the earth gets too hot, they will grow large and cold and ashen as Pluto. They will glow in the dark. And, in times of need, slice the bomb with their sentient hand.

PROMETHEUS REPORT

Do you have the M-T-H-F-R mutation? You know, the "Motherfucker" gene? You can't detox with that one. My sister has it—her liver's heavy with yellow fat. I have the "Warrior" gene, which means I'm reckless and explains my love of over-reaching. Are you of the rs53576 genotype for Optimism and Empathy? Can you accurately read the emotions on the faces of others? Are you less likely to startle when blasted by a loud noise or become stressed at the prospect of such a noise? I'm depressed about my rs1805009 variant. Poor tanning ability. Thank goodness I have the "Speech Impediment" variant to offset it. My subtle lisp makes me extremely attractive to both men and women. Aw, I'm just fucking with ya. Do you have the "Human Foresight" gene mutation? That means you'll die in a bed of your own making. Dharma had that one. On the day of her death, she used seven yoga mats to cushion her fall.

HOW DRONES ARE BORN

A porcelain doll abandons her carriage and crouches like an insect in the corn. The girl, from her bedroom window, reaches for the doll, but slumps in a white ruffled collar. A wafer of arsenic crosses the sky. Green powder blooms from her mother's dress. A black milk seeps from the child. Her father, in his rocking chair on the lawn, bites his fat tongue in the dark. All night, the doll waltzes through the corn until dawn erases her face. Blades sprout from her neck and she ascends into the cracked clouds.

UNWILLING ROBOT

I wasn't prepared
for my current state
of wakefulness. My soul

sits patiently in a chair.
In this way, my body
is a waiting room,

a fish tank, a box of static.
For what am I
halfway through my life,

if not my shadow
reaching the mailbox
long before me.

DEAR LIFE FORM

You will believe you are traveling down a throat of stars. In severe cases, it will dissolve your organs in less than six minutes. Watch for warning signs: a constant ache around the eyes, fits of sleeping and waking, the urge to "clown around." If you think you are a civil service worker, you may already be. We predict a band of searing winds will toast you in your sleep. Do not be alarmed. We've avoided sickness by wearing festive kitchenware: turkey basters, corncob holders shaped like little corns. We've painted big red sores across our bare chests. We've run amok among the AstroTurf! We've even smoked our rabbits, Alice and Earl. However, our third and brightest rabbit, Phil, has grown a curious eight feet in a matter of hours. He's in the parlor with me now, dictating this memo and stroking a dawn horse, braying in the palm of his paw.

BINDING SPELL

I make a doll of you. I make a doll of me. I stuff us full of feathers, fingernails and fur. Stitching us up, I drop a dollop of blood in our trunks. I light a candle with a lock of your hair, sprinkle salt. I coat our poppets with oil and slip your little wooden hand up my woolen skirt. Pinch my tiny nipples with clothespins. I strike our sex parts together like flints and say, Anima Animus, this is how we truss, truss, truss. I wire our wrists, our knees, our navels, our tongues, our flirting shadows. I pierce your red wax heart with a bouquet of pins. I fasten the exact angle our last breaths intersect on the Table of Improbable Sums. I hobble you. I drive a nail through us both. Forgive me, beloved. If only I could keep you in a chair by my side, always forming a word, I'd refrain from cutting off your hands and stitching them in reverse. I know it hurts to bear your palms to the world. There's no better way to reach me when I'm burning on the other side.

NOT A POLE-VAULTING ROBOT

I turn my head to the window and a piece of foil lilting across the onion field. If I were a pole-vaulting robot, I wouldn't be thinking about snowstorms or my stiffening hands. I wouldn't fixate on my giant-heavy head or these yellow, watery eyes. No, if I were a pole-vaulting robot, I'd run so fast my legs would become invisible. I'd beat my shiny cold chest and make thunder. I'd be seduced by pageantry, white kites and waving. They jump for the fame, you know. And they know it's a sin, but without their adoring fans, pole-vaulting robots would be nothing but cans crying into themselves.

ICESCAPE

I'm in a line of people snaking far into the distance. When I look around, I notice everyone's eyes are enormous black pearls. *Why doesn't anyone have color in their eyes?* I ask the woman standing next to me. *Because our pupils are all the way open,* she says. Suddenly, we are sitting in red chairs. We are a long bloody vein stretched over ice. *Why are we sitting?* I ask the woman. *From time to time we are allowed to sit,* she says. Finally, I hear my name boom so loudly it echoes off the ice. I jump up, but so does everyone else. I raise my hand, wave it around wildly and yell, *It's me! It's me!* But everyone does the same. After a few minutes of silence and looking around at each other in a brand-new confusion and adversarial system, we all sit back down. The sun never rises or falls again. Each century is the same shade of yellow.

SNOWGLOBE

For days, I waded through snowdrifts, holding moose antlers above my head. I caught voles, slid their bodies onto the points and stacked them neatly as hors d'oeuvres. After a time, I carved an entire Magic Kingdom of Ice to guard against the starved and directionless. Sometimes, I can hear them calling my name on the snowmobile trails, through the bent spruce and balsam firs. *Wendy, Wendy! Come home, Wendy, we forgive you!* But they are liars. Something thin and cold like a wafer breaks inside me. There is a deep trembling. Then everything goes white again.

PHANTASMAGORIA

It's quieter here in the house, fewer voices, just the occasional startle
of melting snow falling from the eaves like bodies.

They say all bodies are composed of gossamer films. Each time
you photograph one, an actual layer of skin, so thin you can't see it,
is removed and transferred to the photograph.

Likewise, if you stare too long at a photo with longing in your heart,
a spectral layer peels itself from the image and works its way like a worm
into the eye—that sentinel organ between matter and spirit,
between sleeping and waking.

I wonder if that's why I dream of my dead father half in the past,
half in the present, his artist eye wandering into a milky cloud of ectoplasm.

Have I created these fibrous webs, or have they created me?

I've taken too many pictures of the cows in the back field. They look
weak, thin, and seem to be fading into the snowpack.

They say a woman in the throes of lovemaking must not look upon
an image of a beast, not even a pastoral painting hanging by the bed,
lest her child be born with hooves instead of hands.

Inside me, a menagerie of cows.

Once, my lover who died in a housefire came to me in a dream, eyelashes
burned to the quick, ice blue eyes bluer than before. We talked.

It's so quiet tonight I hear the faint clatter of cow bells. Funny thing,
there are no cows in the field, haven't been for years.

They say our words, our actions, even our thoughts imprint
on the picture gallery of the universe—a permanent record
on a great canvas to be judged by a greater Being.

Are those stars or holes in the canvas shielding us from a terrible light?

Sometimes, when I'm sleeping, a voice barks at me from outside
the dream, from the room I'm dreaming inside. It's so loud I wake
with my hand on my ear, no body next to mine.

All things shed themselves and recollect inside us. A cow, for example,
is always emitting a transparent copy of itself, fluid-like, through the air
and into the eye where it materializes into a tiny replica.

In dreams these films collide, mingle. All my dead merge into one
hybrid body. There is a deep and constant lowing from the field.

SPRING COMES

Finally, a woman barges into the house and barks at us to follow. She's making a movie. We hike through the woods to a huge, frozen lake coated with snow. She says, *go*. We obey. *Is this far enough? No*, she says, *go farther*, and we do. When we get to the center, her voice is small and tin. *Now, make snow angels*, and we do. We lie under the star-built sky. Our wings glinting like axes. Then the moon begins to swing back and forth as if hung from a chain. Back and forth, back and forth, through the whole length of the sky, growing bigger and brighter and brighter. We are hypnotized. We are harrowed. We are hacking the ice for our hearts.

THE LOOKING-GLASS PLANET

The wounded deer dragging its fainting limbs to some untrodden brake,
there to gaze upon the arrow which had pierced it, and to die,
was but a type of me.

—Mary Wollstonecraft Shelley

COPILOT

One by one, we blow them off the highways with our lady-colored laser gun. She has no sense of balance and hangs upside down from a handrail in our cockpit. *Sit down, I say. Your baby-doll dress is blocking my vision. They're getting away in their tan sedans!* She looks at me with these vacant animal eyes and says, *It's time. Listen for the gales, the trumpets, the tambourines. Tambourines?* I ask. She settles into her seat with a rattle. Then, as if she were actually a doll, her eyes close on recline. Leaning near to cup my ear, she whispers, *think stars, no, think star nurseries, think infancy gospels, think trees ripped from their roots and everywhere—windows.*

Day 1: Suddenly aware of our atmosphere suits, the twisted elevator sunk in the dunes, she opens the sleeper units. We scamper past the containment field, past the children and lions guarding the fluid. We find the General. He looks gobbled. She pulls him from the canal like a white spider. Leaves him glistening in starlight.

Day 3: A drone drifts over, dragged by a bouquet of balloons. Our messages to Sunflower Restoration Unit go unanswered. *You promised me the occupation was sound,* I said. She pretends not to hear me and weaves us tunics out of vines and red berries. At night, after long treks in the heat, we eat the fizzy fruit from each other's bodies until our dark mouths leak and we nod off.

Day 6: I turn my stitches to the moon.

Day 14: We are topless. We still cannot access the fluid. And how the dry brush feels like razors when the wind kicks up. And how the sand and wind rage. And how the sky and wind and our bony arms wrapped around each other and the new world everlasting turns ashen. And how the days grow dark-eyed, bifocaled. How she fixates on clouds and her longing for flight. How I see nothing but the little noose swaying deep in the pupil of her eye. As if on a screen, it flickers on then off then on then off.

Day 26: My nail beds begin to bleed. She vomits glitter.

Day 40: We blind what birds we can.

Day 43: We lose each other in the sandstorm. I hear her savage call. I want to tell her shhh, I'm here where you left me, in the blue basin, waiting to catch your failing analogue heart like an egg from the sky.

Day 50: Two ruddy suns set upon a stretcher. Like trumpet flowers, we descend into reverie, sink our claw boots into the cracks and take hold.

Day 53: What if she is the machine that programmed this world and the machine that unplugs this world, leaves me a husk in coarse grass, dreaming of a harp adrift on a raft.

Day 77: How like a parable of forgotten is the sound of flight.

Day 80: A tiny golden contraption on my knee. Outside, the rain turns septic in the battlefield clouds. Inside the contraption, a soft pink gear pulsates. When they come to administer the fluid, I hide the contraption in my ear, which is how I come to hear the argument inside each flower: *There never was a war, lumbering dirigible, or shattered biosphere. Only a girl who turned into a bird and flew next to you for a time.*

Acknowledgments

Grateful acknowledgment is made to the editors of the following publications where these poems or versions of these poems first appeared:

Aperçus: "Barn Burning," "Bunny Woman," "Icescape," "Life Form," "Sculpture Garden," "Snuff Poem," "The Vast Wide-Open Space Area"

Apocalypse Now: Prose and Poetry from the End of Days, an anthology by Upper Rubber Boot Press: "Copilot," "Icescape," "Life Form"

Bateau: "How Drones are Born," "In Back of the Liquor Store"

Conduit: "Belief is a Default Setting"

Crazyhorse: "My Father's Paintbox"

Entropy: "The Killing Show," "The President's Dream," "Alice's MMA Fight with the President," and "Field Trip to the White House"

FENCE Magazine: "Uncanny Valleys"

Ghost Town: "On the Day of your Wedding," "Invitation," "Unwilling Robot," "A Snowman is Crying Tears of Fire"

Hobart: "Transhuman Devotion," "Overcome," "Postcard from the Coffin," "The Inside-Out"

Interrupture: "Binding Spell"

Iterant: "How Rabbits Finally Took Over the World," "Get Back"

The Museum of All Things Awesome and Go Boom, an anthology by Upper Rubber Boot Press: "Not a Pole-Vaulting Robot"

Painted Bride Quarterly: "Compound," "Matchmakers"

The Rupture: "The Island of Zerrissenheit"

Salt Hill: "Spring Comes, "The Gift"

Sentence: "Welcome to the Dollar Store"

Sixth Finch: "All I Want for Now"

VERSE: "Not a Pole-Vaulting Robot"

A huge, heartfelt thank you to the constellation of friends who offered insights and encouragement on the work: Janet Bowdan, Stella Corso, Amy Dryansky, Corwin Ericson, Herman Fong, Marie Gauthier, Ellen Goldstein, James Grinwis, Daniel Hales, Lauren Henley, Elizabeth Hughey, Christopher Janke, Daniel Mahoney, Sean Murphy, Janel Nockleby, Catherine Prendergast, Karen Skolfield, Christopher Spencer, Chad Sweeney, Michelle Valois, Diana Whitney, and Matthew Zapruder.

Infinite love and gratitude to my advanced readers who wrote the most generous blurbs a poet could ask for—Chad Sweeney, Matthea Harvey, and Lisa Olstein.

Special thanks to Corwin Ericson, Lauren Henley, Daniel Mahoney, and Chad Sweeney for giving me perspective on the book's message and helping to craft such an amazing description!

My sincere gratitude to everyone at Tupelo Press for the enormous care they put into preparing this book for its journey through the world, especially Jeffrey Levine, Kristina Marie Darling, Cassandra Cleghorn, David Rossitter, and Ann Aspell.

For the gift of time, space and community, thank you Justen Ahren, Founder and Director of the Noëpe Center for Literary Arts on Martha's Vineyard. Thank you and miss you Noëpe family!

Profoundest gratitude to my forever teachers: Agha Shahid Ali, Charles Fort, Megan Macomber, Vivian Shipley, Jim Tate, and Dara Wier for their incredible and enduring generosity, wisdom, and inspiration. My heart to yours.

Thank you, dearest Suzie Ferguson, my Bridge over Troubled Water. To the moon and back and back again!

Thank you to my mother, Lorraine Bock, my Tree of Life, I love you more!

And my biggest thanks to Geoffrey Kostecki, Love of my Life and Secret Weapon.

RECENT AND SELECTED TITLES FROM TUPELO PRESS

Lost, Hurt, or in Transit Beautiful (poems) by Rohan Chhetri

Glyph: Graphic Poetry=Trans. Sensory (graphic poems) by Naoko Fujimoto

Bed (poems) by Elizabeth Metzger

Ashore (poems) by Laurel Nakanishi

The Pact (poems) by Jennifer Militello

Music for Exile (poems) by Nehassaiu deGannes

Nemerov's Door (essays) by Robert Wrigley

Shahr-e-jaanaan: The City of the Beloved (poems)
    by Adeeba Shahid Talukder

I Will Not Name It Except To Say (poems) by Lee Sharkey

The Earliest Witnesses (poems) by G.C. Waldrep

Master Suffering (poems) by CM Burroughs

And So Wax Was Made & Also Honey (poems) by Amy Beeder

The Nail in the Tree: Essays on Art, Violence, and Childhood
    (essays/visual studies) by Carol Ann Davis

Exclusions (poems) by Noah Falck

Arrows (poems) by Dan Beachy-Quick

Salat (poems) by Dujie Tahat

Lucky Fish (poems) by Aimee Nezhukumatathil

boysgirls (hybrid fiction) by Katie Farris

America that island off the coast of France (poems)
    by Jesse Lee Kercheval

Hazel (fiction) by David Huddle

What Could Be Saved: Bookmatched Novellas & Stories
    (fiction) by Gregory Spatz

Native Voices: Indigenous American Poetry, Craft and Conversation
    (poetry and essays) CMarie Fuhrman, Dean Rader, editors

Dancing in Odessa (poems) by Ilya Kaminsky

Xeixa: Fourteen Catalan Poets (poems) edited by Marlon L. Fick and
    Francisca Esteve

Flight (poems) by Chaun Ballard

Republic of Mercy (poems) by Sharon Wang

See our complete list at tupelopress.org